BRAND AUTONOMY

A COLLECTION OF TIPS AND TECHNIQUES
TO HELP ATTRACT MORE USERS TO YOUR
SOFTWARE-AS-A-SERVICE PLATFORM

FRANK DAPP*AH*

AUTHOR OF "PEOPLE-POWERED"
AND "STARTUP MONDAY"

Copyright © 2012 Ostrich press

All rights reserved.

ISBN: 9798747558267

BRAND AUTONOMY

FRANK DAPPAH

OSTRICH®

CONTENTS

	Introduction	15
1	The "selling" side	21
2	A simple idea	25
3	All of the above	28
4	Assembly line	32
5	One of many	40
6	Recurring dream	43
7	Value, not cheap	48
8	Fast learner	54
9	Premium packaging	61
10	Your cup of tea	68
11	Nooks & crannies	77
12	Preaching to the choir	84

13	Something for something	92
14	Thank you	104

A Note to You, the Reader

As a small business owner and entrepreneur, I have been blessed to be able to make a living based on the income earned from doing what I love the most: Building my business and investing in others. Along this wonderful journey that is my (young) life, I have had the pleasure of being in the presence of many truly inspiring people, both young and seasoned.

The work I have done, since the age of 27, when I left the corporate world to pursue my dream of being an entrepreneur – for better or worse – has exposed me to many different experiences, opportunities, and failures.

In this book, as I often do, I will share outcomes of investment/business growth and/or acquisition strategies, tips, insights, and advice.

Though most of these may have resulted in not-so-bad, or good outcomes, others have resulted in substantially adverse consequences.

With that in mind, I want to be clear that I am not a licensed business coach, financial professional, or legal strategist.

I am merely a student and observer of the business world. And while I am more than happy to share what I have learned from my experiences, none of the information I share with you is intended, nor should be construed, to be professional financial or business advice.

If you need help in these areas, consult area-specific professionals.

Neither I nor my publisher is responsible for anything that happens in your own professional and/or business life – good or bad- as a result of doing what I advise in this book.

In fact, these are just my thoughts and experiences and should be treated as such.

Good luck
Frank

"Business opportunities are like buses, there's always another one coming."

-Richard Branson

INTRODUCTION

SIGN OF CHANGE

There really hasn't been a time like this before. Not for a while. Not since the dot-com boom of the mid to late '90s. Not since then has there been such a period of change. Change in the way we interact with one another.

Change in the way we buy things and how we pay for them. Change in what it means to be an investor. Change in what we consider money, and so on. Thangs are changing rapidly around us. Everything is changing. Change is a good thing. Well, most of the time.

We are all witnessing the coming of a new age. For these reasons and others, tech entrepreneurs around the world now find themselves in a uniquely advantageous position to build products for global consumption.

The software space is and has for a while been undergoing its own metamorphoses. Consumers and business users have for a while now opted to access the platforms, they like on a subscription basis, rather than shell out hundreds, even thousands of dollars for the purchase of their favorite software applications.

We are seeing this shift to the software-as-a-service model even more so these days. With stretched household and corporate budgets, and a need to reduce our (collective) carbon footprint, it seems like most types of software tools can now only be accessed on a subscription basis.

Being a fanatical user of tools like Salesforce, all things Adobe, and others, I am immensely appreciative of this shift.

Of course, this migration to service-based applications means that now more than ever, almost anyone can build a successful business or two based on some type of software offering.

I once had a conversation with an aspiring software entrepreneur. And in this conversation, I informed the young lady who was worried about the cost and the skills she felt were needed to build the application she had just talked to me about that building the app was not my biggest concern.

Much to her astonishment, during our conversation/pitch meeting, I seemed less worried about the specific features she was pitching and more concerned with three basic questions:

3) Who is the intended audience for this

app and what problem does the app solve for that person?

2) How many of them are there and how are they solving this issue now?

3) How was she going to get those folks to find her app and sign up for it?

Value propositions
My take on this issue is that there are all kinds of software applications out there and billions of potential users for anything your beautiful mind can come up with. As long as your invention serves a purpose.

Whether you are building an app for the business crowd or to be used by consumers, there is always someone out there who will find your app interesting or useful. The challenge is to get that person's attention and to keep it long enough to build/show value.

"Value" in our business means. Does this person think it is worth it to exchange their hard-earned cold cash to have uninterrupted access to your software product?

I think this is the best time to let you know that although I am aware of the variety of monetization models out there in the space. My "expertise" is confined to the pay-for-play side of things.

So, that being said, I figured it would help if I created a book, this book to help share some of the techniques I have used in the past, and still do to tackle the aforementioned challenges.

CHAPTER ONE

THE "SELLING" SIDE

"Brand Autonomy" is indeed my latest attempt to tackle one of the most fundamental challenges every software entrepreneur faces today.

It is quite daunting, as it is, to go out there and build a software application, any software application. Whether for the business crowd or for everyday consumers, it is always a challenge to assemble a set of features that seek to offer intrinsic value to the end-user.

It is equally challenging to position your app in the right medium to allow for maximum usability.

It is said that the now-defunct mobile-only streaming service Quibi's major issue was that, well, it was mobile-ONLY. The creators of what I personally thought was a pretty cool service, one that I would have paid for had it not been confined to my mobile device, did not anticipate that most folks would want to watch TV on a, ahem! TV.

Slate of original shows from Quibi

In all seriousness, there are many challenges to getting it right in the software arena, or any business for that matter.

I happen to think that most software entrepreneurs, because software folks tend to be more technical types of folks, rarely consider the "selling" aspect of their creations.

In other words, they, software entrepreneurs, coders, techies, whatever you want to call them, tend not to have plans on how to get folks to sign up for their apps.

And to have a set of scenarios that lead to actually collecting payment from their users. In this book, I share a few of the techniques I use to do just that.

CHAPTER TWO

A SIMPLE IDEA

Is there money to be made in the world of software? Of course, there is. Software is everywhere these days. Gone are the days when the word itself: "software", struck fear in the hearts of those of us who are not coders/developers.

It was inconceivable, not too long ago, for a guy like me – a non-technical person – to try to build a wholly-owned software company. But that is what I did. That is what I do (for a living). Our company develops software tools to help sales teams acquire and manage customers.

We never, as a company, set out to build a software division. We always viewed this space as reserved for a select few who had the skills and savvy to pull such a thing off.

We all (my team) come from the era when a few organizations bought enterprise software. And even fewer sold these types of tools. These were large organizations with vast distribution networks and even larger production facilities.

I am talking about the names we all know and love. The Microsofts, the Adobes, and so on.

CHAPTER THREE

ALL OF THE ABOVE

By the way, I will be using the word "sell" or "selling" quite a bit during our time together. I shall do so for two main reasons:

1) I am a sales guy. It is, therefore, natural for me to look at every opportunity to connect with others, existing customers, potential investors, etc. as a selling opportunity.

2) Probably, more importantly, I shall resort to the excessive use of this word so as to help you wrap your head around the idea that nothing in this world "sells itself". They will not come just because you built it.

Many, many, coffee shops and bars

around the world are filled with failed software entrepreneurs who found themselves at a standstill as far as their business prospects go for having this same false sense of how the marketplace, any market works.

No matter what you are offering, you will have to convince folks to try your solution and make it easy for them to do just that.

In other words, regardless of your product type or category, you must have a plan to sell your stuff to your potential customers.

And in my experience, the fewer hurdles there are to folks getting to experience the magic of your product, the better.

This is one of the reasons why, while email verification is still a common practice in our business, most modern applications log the user directly into the platform only to have said user verify their credentials upon later access.

This is to make sure that the user does not have to wait, go find the verification email in order to enjoy the application and its features. Keep that tip in your back pocket. It makes a world of a difference in your user acquisition numbers.

So, where was I? Oh yes, these days, everything we consume, it seems, is software or is somehow made possible through the magic of technology.

Our insatiable appetite for all things tech presents various opportunities for you, regardless of how niche your app may be, to go out and attract the right users.

BRAND AUTONOMY

CHAPTER FOUR

ASSEMBLY LINE

The software or software-as-a-service (SaaS) ecosystem has evolved, over time, to become this super dynamic, multifaceted one.

Given the recent rise in the adoption of apps like Robinhood, the popular investing app. And Coinbase, the cryptocurrency marketplace, and the entire Decentralized finance (Defi) space, the software arena has become a giant entity onto itself.

Netflix recently announced that it plans to spend roughly $17 billion in 2021 towards the acquisition and development of new content. And of course, the streaming giant's rivals plan to make similar moves in the years to come.

Consumers today, really all folks, are constantly glued to some type of screen. It is estimated that the average person spends about 24 hours a week on screens.

Between our computers, smart televisions, and mobile devices, it seems folks today do most of their "living" in some type of digital format.

Among the many beneficiaries of these trends is all things software. In 2020 alone, the SaaS space generated over $105 billion in revenue.

Experts expect the space to continue to grow with more entrants into the space. For the year 2022, the industry it expected to generate global revenue of over $140 billion.

Mergers and acquisitions

In these times, just about anyone can get into this business. All one needs is the desire to succeed. Of course, basic business principles still apply here. But you already know that don't you?

I am sure you are an enterprising person with the skills and aptitude to make things happen.

And for said things to happen, you will need a way to acquire the most consequential asset your software business will ever have. That is the app itself.

At our company, Corvus Web Services, we offer various apps. There are many, scratch that, most software operations offer various platforms and tools. All, however, started with one app.

Did you know that the very first Microsoft offering was not one built by the duo – The late Paul Allen and Bill Gates? According to an account by Gates himself, their first product was a result of the rebranding of someone else's operating system.

I say that to say this. There are many ways to get your company's first app even if you are not a software developer. For one, you can for sure hire someone else to build one for you.

The internet is filled with marketplaces where folks like you and I can find coders/software developers who will build exactly the kind of software tool we can dream of.

With the recent popularization of the Application Programming Interface (API) technology and others, you can put together a very robust app. For a fraction of previous costs.

Alternatively, you can always acquire an already built tool from sites like Flippa or Microacquire. Here, you can go the pricier direction and get an app that already has users and brings in money or buy a newly built one that has little traction and grow the user base. I have had success pursuing either option.

Beast mode

One of the major upsides to buying an already developed app, one that you can customize and add more features, is that the developer, the original guy or gal who built it can provide support as you grow your team and users.

This is a move that will as they say, kill two birds with one stone. You will have managed to bring on, even if on a part-time basis, both a tech support person and someone who can potentially build more apps for your young company. You can always add to the team as your business grows. For now, you will have the free time to focus almost entirely on acquiring new users.

That is the first reason. The second is that the architect of the app, your new app, would have, should have worked their way through most of the debugging steps typically needed.

This will save you a ton of cash and save you from the stress of supporting an app with many bugs.

The most important reason of all is that this app would have already started its way through the various milestones you will proceed to try to hit in order to become profitable as a company/app.

You will of course, among many

benchmarks, try to get your first 100 (free) users. This particular milestone is one of import in our industry.

And thus, should be on the list of your first things to do. Some folks I have worked with in the past, will go out and try to raise some cash for the main purpose of marketing their new app on platforms like Facebook, Google, and Twitter. That works well too.

CHAPTER FIVE

ONE OF MANY

One of the things, well, two things I would love to stress to you. Especially if you are new to this (software-as-a-service) business is to first not look at the successful acquisition of free trial users as a victory on its own. Sure, it is a step in the right direction. One of many.

Many software entrepreneurs get caught up in this mindset.

Unless your business model will rely heavily on selling ads based on the number of eyeballs your app has, like Facebook, or Twitter, then I recommend that you see your ability to acquire free users – The folks who are willing to take a moment to sign up for your app – as merely the opening to a conversation.

Perhaps you should look at it as a first date. On the first date, back in my day at least, folks were there to check out what the other person had to offer. Kind of "ok, you got my attention. I'm listening" type of stance.

If you liked what you heard, you moved on to the next step. To me, this is what a free trial user is.

It is then incumbent on you to prove, during the free trial phase, that your app is worth buying/subscribing to.

CHAPTER SIX

RECURRING DREAM

This brings me to the next point I wanted to make in this two-part drama. That is to know how to ask for the money. In face-to-face sales or telesales, you take a more direct approach.

In software sales, however, you must lay the psychological groundwork and work out the "convenience" factor in ways that encourage folks to hand over the money.

Regardless of your approach to marketing, onboarding, and so forth.

Before we take all these actions that will (potentially) allow new users to find and signup for your software-as-a-service platform, you must first decide where you fit into your chosen marketplace.

For example, Skype, the popular team collaboration and telephony tool, is not unique in what it does. The Microsoft-owned application, however, appeals to the lower end of the market in terms of pricing. And also, to an international audience.

Most of the folks I do business with overseas use Skype for their business communications.

The monthly cost for having Skype and all of its business-enabled features is around $2.99. A far cheaper price than say a Slack or Asana.

For skype users such as myself, the low cost is one of the main reasons we use it – Among other things.

So, in the vast marketplace, which is

the one you will compete in, you must first clearly decide which end of the market your app will be in. And it is a marketplace, you know?

There are various potential users out there who, by the way, are not a monolith.

Your users will come in all shapes and sizes with varying needs.

You must not fall into the trap of trying to build features to satisfy all the potential needs of all of the folks you are trying to sign up as users.

These actions can ultimately render your app clunky and complicated.

You must also be aware of the various competitors out there. Some of which will have a better understanding of the market than you. Most will, let's face it, have a better product than yours when your start out.

But that is ok. There is always

someone out there for you. This is true in both life and business. Your goal is to (first) find those users that are best suited for your app.

As you work to develop your unique selling proposition(s), among many other things, let me spend the next few chapters sharing with you some of the ways you can go about positioning your offer to acquire free and subsequently, paying customers.

CHAPTER SEVEN

VALUE, NOT CHEAP

In my humble opinion, one of the greatest misconceptions in our industry, the software industry, and most industries for that matter is that "Value = Cheap". I used to think this way too – if I am being honest.

It would take me years of working in sales to realize that "value" can mean vastly different things to different people.

To a guy or gal who can afford to and is paying $100 per month for a great CRM system, offering a similar product that has the core features they need and that gets less expensive as they add new users and/or customers, will present great value.

Value, the way I see it – in this case – should be presented as a way of offering your well-defined audience a platform that meets their core needs for less than what your competition is charging.

Most businessfolk act as if this is some kind of taboo subject. Most people I know, for some reason, dislike talking about what I feel is one of the most important elements that drive mankind's spending habits. We all go out to buy what we need looking to get the most value for our money.

For this reason, you should pay a great deal of attention to the overall pricing dynamics in your niche and try to, with your team, develop a pricing strategy that will allow you to stay competitive while being profitable.

Race to the bottom

As a small company, your firm is in a great position to present itself as the *Value player* in your niche. With a small, more focused operation, you will be able to communicate to the marketplace as also reflected in your pricing that yours is the platform to use while on a tight budget. There is no shame in being known as the "cheaper alternative" in your space.

I will caution you though not to fall into the trap of simply mimicking your competitors' product and/or features and just slapping a cheaper price on your stuff.

In other words, your pitch cannot, and should not be "Hey, we are just like Slack, but cheaper" This presents many challenges to you and your businesses.

For starters, most folks will then make their decision to switch to or go with your product based purely on a dollar-to-convenience calculus.

The question you will force your potential users to ask is, "is it worth switching to save XYZ dollars?". And we know most folks put a premium on convenience. In fact, this is one of those main drivers of spending we will talk about later in this book.

You would have put yourself in a position where you are forcing folks to put a price on convenience. And for a company of 12 that has been using Slack for the last six years, asking them to switch to a cheaper, unproven alternative just to save a few dollars will not make sense.

For those potential users out there, who have not made up their minds about one SaaS platform or another, you will then put them in a position to decide between both products based on whether being on a pricier but more widely used platform is worth paying the extra bucks.

And your lesser-known app will lose that battle every single time. Also, pricing your app just to undercut the next guy puts your entire industry in a "race to the bottom" mode. This is where folks will go out to acquire new customers with deep, profit-busting discounts and promotions. This is good for no one.

Well, except the end-user. This is certainly not good for a new business such as yours.

In this battle, your relatively weak financial position, as well as your lack of brand authority, will put you at a disadvantage.

CHAPTER EIGHT

FAST LEARNER

Alternatively, offering / positioning your Pay-as-you-go software application as the "value" choice will put you and your firm in various advantageous positions.

You will be able to start to grow your user base at a more rapid pace than that of your larger competitors.

This will help you get a better understanding of your niche and the entire market as a whole.

You will be able to appeal to smaller companies. That is if your application fits into the so-called Business-to-business (B2B) category.

For example, the average user for any of our apps is a company of 1 – 5 people. We, Corvus Web Services, live at the lower end of the market. This is our core user base. And it works well for us.

The comment section.
You will be able to sign up more budget-conscious consumers if your app is meant to be used by the general public. This puts your firm in the "new high growth" category.

You don't need me to tell you that this new moniker will help you get more media attention and enable you to raise more investor capital.

You will also have access to these

new users and their opinions about your application and other similar platforms.

Not to mention the intelligence derived from studying how folks use your tool and its features.

For what you lose in profit margins on account of your average user paying less than that of your more established competitors, you will gain invaluable feedback.

Not an either or

At the cash register at my neighborhood Wal-Mart, I said to the friendly Ethiopian lady, *"I didn't think you guys got this busy on a Monday"* She looked at me as if she did not quite catch what I had just said.

And so, I repeated what was my pathetic attempt at small talk. She kind of cut me off almost as if her brain had just connected what I was about to say and the bits and pieces she gleaned from the last thing I had said and replied (with a smile), *"oh yeah! We get busy after 9 am and it stays this way till around 2 pm"*.

"Wow. I try to avoid Wal-Mart unless I have to buy a lot of stuff" I replied.

Then she looked at me while bagging what was obviously an unhealthy amount of chicken tenders and asked, *"Where else do you go?"*. *"Harris Teeter"* I said.

I told her this is where I go for the everyday stuff and although she reminded me how expensive the Teet – as nobody calls it – was, I told her I did not mind the cost in those moments.

I tell you this story because as uneventful as this interaction may seem, a valuable aspect of consumerism is inadvertently revealed.

In all honesty, since I work from home, I was just trying to interact with another human. It was natural for me to talk to this lady because we both come from the motherland.

That being said, I had shown myself to be a consumer of more than one brand for the same need. The difference being that I got to one place for convenience and the other for value.

For value, I am willing to sometimes give up convenience. And vice versa.

You should not come to view your users as one homogeneous group but rather as a dynamic plethora folks with varying needs and wants.

Language of value
No matter one's background, needs, or budget, we all sometimes choose value. It is important for you to also place yourself in a position and your team as well to try to, develop the language to try to communicate

your understanding of the complex needs of your users and to use these key points of communication/pitch in your marketing campaigns.

Offering value does not mean that yours is a just a cheap software-as-a-service product. I cannot stress this point enough. Offering value can just be the first step in your journey to building a dynamic software company. One that can grow to offer many different tools and price-points to many different kinds of users.

CHAPTER NINE

PREMIUM PACKAGING

We both know that like most verticals, the software space is filled with a multitude of applications that are built to solve an assortment of different problems.

From platforms that allow you to monitor your vitals to apps that help small businesspeople manage their businesses, the whole "there is an app for that" phraseology is now truer than ever.

As a result of the sheer volume of the various options out there, entrepreneurs who have been trained to believe that being the only vendor of any particular product or service in the marketplace is the ultimate unique selling point, often fret over the perceived lack of opportunities.

In other words, most startup-ers feel that for a business idea to have legs, it must be one that is not currently on the market anywhere. It has to be a unique Software platform that does stuff the likes of which the world has never seen.

Of course, the market itself, any market is the counter argument to this point of view.

Sure, oftentimes, having first-mover advantage can help reap loads of intrinsic benefits. I do not think anyone can deny that. The reality is that these types of opportunities rarely present themselves.

Stepping outside of the SaaS ecosystem, one will notice a number of brand options in almost every product category there is.

Candy store economics

In fact, the availability of options in these various types of stuff we buy is an essential part of every healthy, vibrant marketplace.

A trip to your local deli to buy a sandwich will prove to be one filled with various multiple-choice questions.

There will be choices made involving the type of bread you want, the type of cheese, sauces, and so on.

This is one of those aspects of business that I consider to be ultra-exciting.

The software-as-a-service arena is no different. One must venture to build products to capture a subsegment of a defined audience.

Though how you choose to approach this issue has many sides, one other proven theme to help attract users to your SaaS app – even if you are in a crowded market – is by being the "Premium" vendor in your chosen category. Or at least one of them. Unlike in the cases where you propose to be the discount/value vendor.

A strategy that relies heavily on your ability to attract a large number of paying users. Being the premium option ventures to bring in fewer but higher dollar users.

You will, however, be able to go beyond the core features of your app to fulfill your promise and perhaps justify your price points.

The economics of premium

Of course, you will not want to market your app as being one for premium users. That would be obnoxious. The thing about the premium services we all use is that we know and tell our friends that these services are more geared towards "premium users" based on our experiences with said service/company.

For years, folks paid $10 more on their cable bills for HBO, not simply because the network, via the cable vendors demanded it. Nope!

They instead marketed great, unique shows, gave users free trials, employed various marketing schemes to communicate this idea and let customers decide for themselves if they felt the content, they were able to access was worth the extra cash.

Even today, I still pay extra for HBO via my Amazon Prime account so I can watch shows like *Mare of Easttown* and Regina King's *Watchmen*.

You must employ similar tactics to enhance your position in the marketplace as the "Premium option".

Going beyond features

The reality is that in the "features" area, it would be exceedingly difficult to compete or be unique.

I mean, how many other ways can you design a Contact management system that has not already been done?

What else can an email marketing

platform do that would be so far beyond providing users the tools to help them manage email campaigns?

Most of these applications will have similar features. You, my friend, will not be able to re-invent the wheel here.

In the software space, it is hard to differentiate yourself and command higher dollars via your application's features alone.

I have found that what you do outside of the app itself is what will make you stand out. Companies like Constant Contact, for example create unique experiences for their users via their award-winning customer service.

ZoomInfo, the business data vendor has a very easy-to-use platform plus a great onboarding process that makes it easy for any type of user to get up and running in no time.

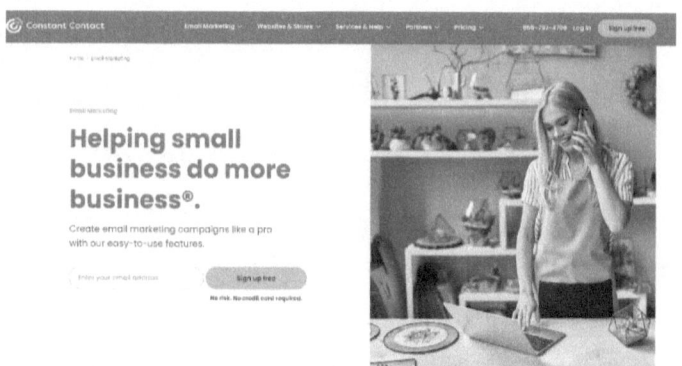

https://www.*constantcontact.com/email-marketing*

CHAPTER TEN

YOUR CUP OF TEA

Your value proposition will be most felt in the way you build your features and app and what features you include.

But customer support, Sales and promotions, user onboarding, and so on. These are the things that when done to meet the unique needs of your users will make the difference.

But to do so, we must first get an understanding of the needs of our potential users.

Guided flight

One of the consequences of having a totally open and global marketplace, one filled with small businesses, even more so than larger corporations and organizations, is the diversity of potential users and customers out there.

Whether your SaaS platform will be for use by businessfolk or consumers, you must understand that your users will hail from all four corners of the world and have all sorts of needs and culture-based expectations.

Your business-to-business app, be it a project management tool or social media management app will be used by all kinds of businesses. Most of these will be small businesses and institutions.

This is to be expected since small businesses, those with 1 -500 employees, make up over 90% of all global businesses.

In the United States, small businesses, 99% of all businesses, are responsible for over 64% of all new jobs created. My point is, if your software application is a business tool, more than likely, you will have "small businesses" as your largest customer base/segment. You must therefore position your business to meet the needs of this unique cross section of the general market.

Global landscape.

I was shocked to learn that most of the readers of these little books that I author in my spare time are actually, according to the data, folks in the United Kingdom. In fact, the U.S is not on the top five list in terms of the countries of origin of my readers.

Our software products are used by folks all over the world. I say all this to let you know that in today's business environment, you must prepare your software tool to support all types of users.

One way to differentiate yourself from your competition, and to command higher subscription revenues is to design your customer support, sales, landing pages, websites, onboarding tutorials and so on, to meet the needs of users at all adoption levels and from various continents.

3) You might want to create your app in such a way that can be easily translated into other popular languages.

2) You might want to, via tools like Upwork, hire sales and customer service folks from various different countries to support folks in corresponding geographies.

3) Establishing your software-as-a-service platform as specific to the needs of niche types of businesses can also help attract premium users. We will get into this a bit more later.

Open door policy

The open-door policy mindset must apply to the way you interact with your team as well as your customers. Larger businesses have no issues including their customers in their decision-making processes. In fact, this has become the norm.

In today's social media-conscious environment, businesses, both large and small, now have various means through which they can gauge the proverbial temperature of both their employees and the general public.

Small businesses, because they are typically built around the personality of one or a few people struggle to include their people and customers in their feedback systems.

What I do every day is try to build a business to support me, my family, my team and most importantly, the businesses of our users and customers. It is therefore imperative that I am paying close attention to what these various stakeholders think and need in order to be successful at what they do. Collecting and implementing the values embedded in feedback, regardless of where said feedback comes from, is always a positive thing.

We hear you.

That being said, taking constant feedback from the folks around you to improve your business/SaaS tool, if not done in an organized way can get messy.

You also run the risk of making changes that add no value or further complicate the entire process of working with your organization and/or using your software application.

Trust me when I tell you that I have been there.

In most cases, we ended up creating complicated applications chocked-full of features that were not consequential to the core functions of our users' businesses.

For these reasons, among others, it is important that you set up unique internal systems to help take incoming feedback, assign a level of importance, design a way to reach out to those responsible for said feedback to convey acknowledgement and to include them in the process of change. Should that be the outcome.

I find it super helpful to assign a team member to the task of sifting through these customer and/or employee feedback to run them through your designed systems. These are but a few ways you, the software entrepreneur, can present unique, premium value to your end-users.

CHAPTER ELEVEN

NOOKS AND CRANNIES

In business, and the software business is no different, opportunities can be found everywhere. Even in the unlikeliest of places.

As I have said before, we are all living in one beautifully- interconnected global economy now.

The software applications we use here in the United States – to run our businesses, to catch up on our favorite shows, etc. – are the same apps being used in Nairobi, Kyiv, Singapore, and elsewhere around the world.

I, on a daily basis, through apps like Skype and WhatsApp, communicate - for business and personal reasons - with folks all around the world. I have folks I speak to in Africa, India, and Europe. I do it all with absolute ease as a result of the various software applications out there. But that is not the point of this conversation.

Inclusive process
That being said, planning to build a software-as-a-service platform, whether for

businessfolk or everyday people, should be planned accordingly.

Again, the purpose of this book was and is to share with you some of the strategies and ways of approaching the all-important "user acquisition" part of your success story.

User acquisition does not start and end with the way you decide to position your app through your sales and marketing efforts.

Nope! The kind of user you hope to attract to use your SaaS platform should be at the top of your mind during every single step of the way.

Even before your write (or pay for someone to write) the first line of code, during the blueprint stage of your app, when your app is just a sketch on a piece of paper, you must be thinking very carefully about who exactly the audience for your application will be.

Every anticipated need must be considered. I sometimes encourage folks to go as far as talking to some of these ideal would-be users on hopes of ascertaining specifically what features to invest in.

Corners of growth

One of the rarely-thought-of ways one such as yourself can position your app to be able to ramp up your user base and also differentiate yourself in the marketplace is by appealing to a niche.

As entrepreneurs and small business owners, we all in one way or the other suffer from this affliction that causes us to want to create products and services for "everyone".

Fear of missing out is but one of the various reasons we think this way. We never stop to think of all those brands that are not well-known to the general public but once you start asking folks in any particular obscure business, they start to rant and rave about products the average person has never even heard of.

Curated spaces

Brain Shark is, to me, one of those types of apps. The Waltham, Massachusetts-based software-as-a-service company creates and markets its applications specifically to help sales organizations create training videos.

One other such tool is Agdata. The Charlotte, North Carolina company creates tools exclusively for the agriculture space. More specifically to help farmers manage their operations.

In the consumer-ready app space, I can think of a few apps that are built to be used by a niche group of users. One that pops into my head as I write these words is

Concord, Los Angeles CA-based Peachy.

The mobile app is meant to be used by medical professionals. The app aims to provide doctors with the tools they need to help streamline payments between their businesses and their patients.

And of course, LinkedIn is probably the best example of a company that successfully carved out a very profitable niche user base in an already crowded space.

We're currently building this product with the following principles in mind:

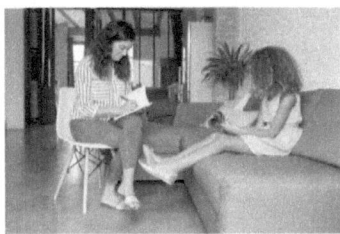

Increased access

Every day, providers miss out on patients who need their services but "can't afford" them. At Peachy, this is unacceptable. To remedy this, Peachy Pay Later helps patients "afford" health care, by allowing them to spread their payments out over months instead of requiring it in one, lump sum payment.

It also allows providers who historically have higher rates of out of network or HSA reimbursement—like therapists, in-patient facilities, and pathologists—to serve more patients. With Peachy Pay Later, providers can get paid upfront, without patients needing to pay in cash, and allow patients to pay off the bill in a manner tailored to their personal situation.

Progressive underwriting

Humane collection practices

Credit Positive

Simultaneously improving the health of patients and providers with easily mobile bill payment.

CHAPTER TWELVE

PREACHING TO THE CHOIR

There are no apps out there that, through its creators, can claim to be perfect. No app leaves no desires, needs, and/or wishes unmet.

Just take a quick trip to the review section of app recommendation sites like AlternativeTo (alternativeto.net) or Startup Ranking (startupranking.com), and one can make an extensive list of the various functions folks wished these, sometimes very well-known apps, did that go beyond their existing core capabilities.

No matter how great a Software-as-a-service application is, there are always going to be some folks out there that would love to see a change here and there.

Folks that wish to see some specific set of features added to said applications.

Open mic night

Now, do not get me wrong. It is true indeed that one can never make everyone happy. Again, you will always have folks that would like to see major minor to major changes made to an app. Any app.

Witnessing various complaints being lobbed at your competitor about the various features of their app, customer service systems, and so forth does not always mean that there is an opportunity for you to take market share.

In fact, a lot of these complaints and feedback are going to be a result of this new dynamic we have where everyone has a voice. You know as well as I do that thanks to the power of social media and the fact that these brands, we all know and love are constantly seeking the public's opinion about all manner of things, folks these days feel the need to provide an endless list of complaints and opinions about almost everything.

There are thousands of YouTube channels out there that do just that. Basically, folks complaining about all types of products and services.

That being said, there are instances where some complaints are ones that can present an opportunity for you as the software entrepreneurs that you are.

Spotting a niche
So, how can one spot legitimate complaints about a specific software application? Well, *volume* is one way to know if an issue about an app can lead to you building something better to acquire users. The sheer volume of complaints is one aspect that can create an

opportunity for you to directly address the needs of a niche.

Then there is the type of complaints that are being made. The idea is to find ways to differentiate between complaints that address a core systemic issue about an app or if these are issues your larger competitor can fix easily to meet the needs of a growing user base.

I will give you one such example. Crypto trading has become one of the hottest trends around these days. The more we hear, on the news, about average Joe's out there becoming millionaires as a result of buying and selling digital currencies, the more average folks want to get into the game.

As a result of this surging demand, there are various outfits out there that have launched software applications to address this demand. The issue at hand as I see it is that most of these so-called crypto trading platforms are complicated as heck to use. I mean, you have to be really tech savvy to navigate the features of these apps. I think Coinbase is probably the most user-friendly among the bunch. But the popular crypto trading app still requires some degree of technological know-how to use (successfully).

In a situation such as these, we know those who build these types of apps are often young, tech savvy dudes.

I mean, let's face it. That is true, right. Tech folks never actually think about the usability of their creations as far as the average man or woman is concerned.

Here is where a person such as yourself can build and market a SaaS app with your main selling point being "ease-of-use". The big guys will not stop to disrupt their businesses just to make a tiny little niche happy. But you can.

Also, you will have to determine if these are issues that make life or work harder for the end user. Or are these just a list of "would be nice if.." complaints.

In other words, we want to know if enough users would be willing to switch apps if these needs were met. You, will have to grab a pen and paper, make a list of these issues and using your best judgement, make various determinations about the best way forward.

Gender bias

With that in mind, there are various groups you can consider when thinking of creating software tools that can be sold to specific niche groups.

Your focus can be directed towards the needs of a gender-based niche. There are many products and services that are built to appeal only to either males or females.

The U.S economy has for decades relied on this element of consumer behavior to grow. From movie makers to tool makers, all types of companies build various versions of their products and services and at times, whole new categories of products to be marketed (exclusively) to either women or men, little girls or boys.

Although the software space has not quite seen this type of phenomenon take hold, there is no reason why you cannot be a trailblazer in this department. You can build your software-as-a-service tools to meet the needs of a targeted gender group.

Same strategy can be adopted to meet the needs of various other groups. Groups such as members of the LGBTQ community, people of color, and so forth.

CHAPTER THIRTEEN

SOMETHING FOR SOMETHING

Throughout this book, I have shared with you some of the ways in which I look at, and approach user acquisition as it relates to the various SaaS applications, we, as a company, operate.

Needless to say, most of the strategies I have talked about can in fact by modified and utilized across various industries.

Regardless of whether you are in the business of selling coffee, or you operate a trucking company, some of the ways in which you can acquire new customers reverberate across various unrelated business types.

For me, there is no aspect of product development, in terms of the Software-as-a-Service space, more important than one's user acquisition plan. In other words, how will you get folks to sign up for your software application? And once you start to gain traction as far as your users go, how do you plan to keep a majority of the folks who signed up for your app?

Of course, as we have talked about, there are many ways in which you can answer these basic questions. Ways that I am sure go far beyond some of the tips I have shared in the conversation we have been having for the past, what? 130 plus pages?

My only wish is that you seriously consider these points and do everything in your power, given your resources, to thoroughly address these issues prior to the commitment of further resources towards the production of your app. And any subsequent marketing and/or sales initiatives.

With all that in mind, over the years, I have stumbled upon a few ways through which - in addition to these overall steps- can help you ramp up your user base in a timely fashion.

Checkout counter

Before we get into the nitty-gritty of some of the basic steps, I think you can take to hasten your user acquisition strategy, I would like you to come along with me on what I anticipate will be a fairly straightforward mental exercise.

I am sure like most red-blooded humans; you have shopped quite a few times for groceries (during your life so far). Perhaps, in your family, you are the main guy or gal who does the grocery shopping.

And if you are the designated grocer in your tribe, well, then you don't need me to tell you what a perilous activity shopping for groceries can be. Those who do it frequently understand the need to plan, strategize and work to execute said plan as impeccably as possible.

Every aspect of one's shopping expedition must be planned in such a way that leaves no detail to chance.

The companies responsible for making and/or marketing the stuff we consume on a daily basis understand the need to supply us with the right produce, in addition to the right incentives, in order for us to shop beyond what we actually need (in most cases).

Outfits like Kroger and Wal-Mart understand that there are certain aspects f the human psyche that make us susceptible to certain kinds of incentives.

This is the reason why most of the stuff we consume based on emotional impulses are typically placed strategically at checkout aisles of grocery stores all across these United States.

When we get bored, and boredom is but one element, we tend to do anything to eliminate the monotony.

There are studies out there that time and time again prove that people will do anything rather than nothing.

Some folks have been even documented as inflicting pain upon themselves rather than sit quietly for a few minutes.

Shopping is also one of those things that we do rather than be without activity.

So, we shop. We buy trashy magazines. We buy candy bars. We buy weird electronic gadgets and a whole bunch of other crap we would not otherwise spend our hard-earned dollars on.

Digital product placement

As an entrepreneur, you should do your best to incorporate this intel, among other insights, into your user acquisition interfaces.

I, for one, have come to visualize that the final payment page of every SaaS application I build in the context of the checkout counter. I also make use of every interaction the free-trial user has with our apps to convey some type of incentive.

Prime Bundles work

My favorite type of incentive has to be "the bundle". I find that since most of your users will have various needs as it relates to the type of software products they use, it would help to provide them with various tools at once.

The idea is to allow them - your free trial users - to realize some type of discounted price, should they choose to stack a few products before they go ahead and click that Upgrade button.

This strategy can greatly help you acquire users at a discounted rate for some new app that you have just launched. Instead of going out there and paying Facebook or Google for click-throughs (and of course you will have to spend some ad dollars too), you can start signing up paid users fairly quickly by bundling this new app with some other popular app you have.

You can also seek out other SaaS entrepreneurs to offer some type of revenue share should they decide to allow their new users to bundle their service with yours.

This is a very simple but potentially

lucrative setup. We saw our annual recurring revenue (ARR) triple when we started offering our users bundles of our various software products.

Of course, the idea, it goes without saying, is to offer deep discounts to your users in exchange for bundling. Amazon actually uses this strategy quite well within their Prime video ecosystem.

I have paid subscriptions to so many channels and streaming services I would have otherwise never agreed to pay for were it not for the fact that Amazon offered discounted pricing as a bundle with other Prime video offerings.

Paying with crypto

Bitcoin, Ethereum, Dogecoin, and the entire digital currency space have exploded in popularity over the past few years. What was once an obscure, mostly tech-dominated topic has now become common parts of the conversations and most importantly, the investment holdings of everyday folks all around the world.

Even grandmas all around the world now know or have some idea what Bitcoin is.

Though there are many elements to the Decentralized finance (Defi) space, most experts and industry watchers predict stability and mass adoption on the horizon. Better put, the crypto world, undeniably, will grow over the next few years.

I foresee a time not too far in the future when we all hold and use digital currencies as part of our daily transactions. Like peer-to-peer payment systems were in the early days, most folks will catch on as time goes on.

With the Launch of Amazon's Vella platform, one that will accept a yet-to-be-named token as payment. And with companies like Tesla and the Home Depot deciding to accept Bitcoin as payment for their products and services, things will get interesting as time goes on.

My thoughts on this issue are that as a Software-as-a-service entrepreneur, it will make sense to distinguish yourself from your competitors by incorporating crypto into your platform.

Using APIs from companies like Coinbase(commerce.coinbase.com), you can easily and fairly quickly start accepting various Crypto currencies as subscription payments for your SaaS application. It always helps if you design your process to offer convenience and some sort of discount should a user opt to pay in crypto.

Some entrepreneurs will opt to store these payments in the crypto used to pay or convert these payments into more stable coins to allow for appreciation in value.

You can also choose to build loyalty among your subscribers by issuing, on a monthly, weekly, annual basis, crypto as a reward for their continued use of your app. There are many ways to use crypto to enhance your user acquisition strategy. Your imagination will be the only conduit needed to access true innovation.

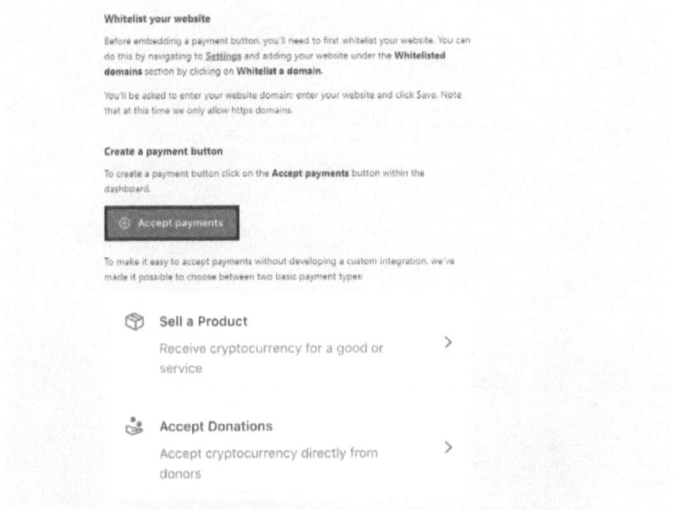

Coinbase API
(https://commerce.coinbase.com/docs/

THANK YOU!

Thank you so much for giving me a chance to be part of your literary/educational diet.

I try to put out books that I think will help provide value to others about various topics that I tell myself I have gained some insight into – or, at the very least, have some experience with.

I often get feedback about the books I, and my publisher, put out. I then use this feedback to improve, and at times, completely change the way I write and/or the topics I write about.

We, and by (we), I mean all of us here at OSTRICH find such feedback extremely useful as we try to carry out our mission to create engaging content.

That being said, please feel free to log onto www.ostrichpress.com or visit our Amazon, Kobo, and Google Play pages to let us know what you think about this book, and any others (from us) you may have read.

And once again, Thank you!

NOTES

https://www.projectmanager.com/blog/30-best-business-quotes

https://www.piesync.com/blog/saas-guide-tools-and-trends/

https://www.esquire.com/entertainment/tv/a32173812/quibi-video-app-shows-short-reviews/

https://www.bmc.com/blogs/saas-growth-trends/#:~:text=Cloud%20growth%3A%20SaaS%20vs%20other%20cloud%20services&text=Gartner%20estimates%20that%20SaaS%20will,generate%20close%20to%20%24141%20billion.

https://www.constantcontact.com/email-marketing

https://www.zoominfo.com/solutions/sales

https://smallbiztrends.com/small-business-statistics#:~:text=What%20percent%20of%20businesses%20are,businesses%20employ%2059.9%20million%20people.

https://www.oberlo.com/blog/small-business-statistics#:~:text=3.-,Small%20and%20Medium%2DSized%20Businesses%20Are%20Major%20Drivers%20of%20Global,a%20large%20number%20of%20jobs.

https://www.worldbank.org/en/topic/smefinance

https://www.vistaequitypartners.com/companies/portfolio/

https://www.agdata.com/solutions/data-management/

https://en.wikipedia.org/wiki/Brainshark

https://www.peachypay.com/solutions/peachy-pay-later

https://alternativeto.net/platform/online/

https://www.startupranking.com/top

https://www.buybitcoinworldwide.com/who-accepts-bitcoin/

https://commerce.coinbase.com/docs/

ABOUT THE AUTHOR

Frank is a serial entrepreneur, author and investor. Frank has written various books on topics like Marketing, social media, entrepreneurship and other areas of business. He resides in Charlotte, North Carolina with his business partner/wife, Bernice.

BRAND AUTONOMY

RECOMMENDED READING

People-powered

Entrepreneurs everywhere - from New York to Nairobi - (often) harbor mixed feelings about their investors. These feelings sometimes veer into the adversarial when there are disagreements about the future of the underlying firm or firms.

Another SaaS (Software-as-a-service) Marketing Book

Another SaaS Marketing Book is a no-fluff practical guide for software developers and entrepreneurs. This book is meant to help shed some light on the many (effective) ways you, as a software entrepreneur can get the word out about your app or business application.

Payment Received: Learn how to successfully launch your Software-as-a-service platform.

Payment Received is one of the best books on SaaS pricing and marketing. In this easy-to-follow book, I lay out a few strategies on how to successfully bring your software-as-a-service or subscription-based app to market.

Find these and many other titles from the author at Amazon.com, Ostrichpress.com, or wherever you buy books.

BRAND AUTONOMY

OSTRICH®

Ostrich Publishers

We love books! It is in our DNA. It is the food we eat and the air we breathe.

We are working hard to build an all-inclusive publishing and distribution platform.

Our Mission

OSTRICH is an all-digital publisher. Our mission is to create a robust medium through which talented independent Authors and Creatives can share their works with the rest of the world.

What We Do

As part of our overall mission, we work closely with authors of all backgrounds to help bring their works to life. Through our robust distribution infrastructure, we can help Authors, who would otherwise go unnoticed, to plan, create and distribute their finished products worldwide. We work with Authors at every step of the process, from brainstorming, to writing, to distribution and marketing. We are working hard to build an all-inclusive publishing and distribution platform.

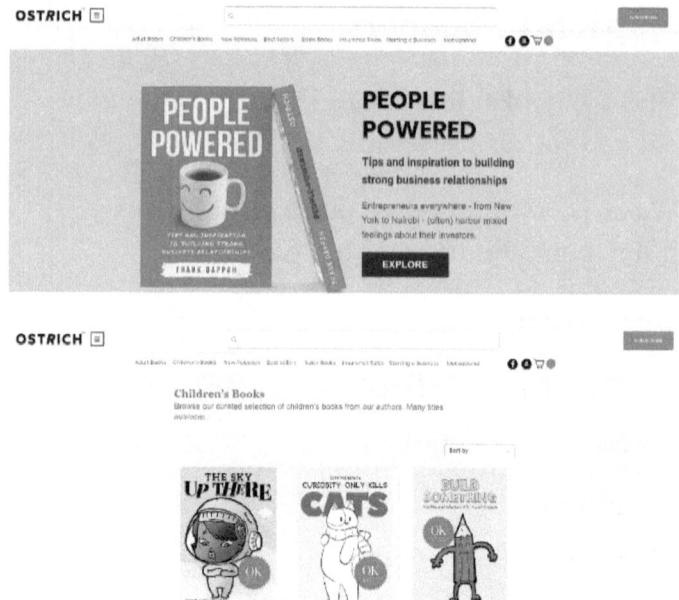

OSTRICH Publishers (https://www.ostrichpress.com/)

BRAND AUTONOMY

A COLLECTION OF TIPS AND TECHNIQUES TO HELP ATTRACT MORE USERS TO YOUR SOFTWARE-AS-A-SERVICE PLATFORM

FRANK DAPPAH

AUTHOR OF "PEOPLE-POWERED" AND "STARTUP MONDAY"

Copyright © 2012 Ostrich press

All rights reserved.

ISBN: 9798747558267

BRAND AUTONOMY

A COLLECTION OF TIPS AND TECHNIQUES TO HELP ATTRACT MORE USERS TO YOUR SOFTWARE-AS-A-SERVICE PLATFORM

FRANK DAPPAH

AUTHOR OF "PEOPLE-POWERED" AND "STARTUP MONDAY"

BRAND AUTONOMY

A COLLECTION OF TIPS AND TECHNIQUES TO HELP ATTRACT MORE USERS TO YOUR SOFTWARE-AS-A-SERVICE PLATFORM

FRANK DAPP*AH*

AUTHOR OF "PEOPLE-POWERED" AND "STARTUP MONDAY"

www.ingramcontent.com/pod-product-compliance
Lightning Source LLC
Chambersburg PA
CBHW020431220526
45464CB00002B/658